Have thumb, will travel

By

Peter Anderson

Edited by Peter Canham

Front cover by Carole Gonzalez

A special thanks to my good friend, fly fishing companion, and editor, Peter. For his friendship, wise council, and work on the book.

Introduction and dedication to Lennie Rook

The idea of writing this book came about as a result of my friendship with a lovely fella called " Lennie Rook" I got to know Lennie when I rented a cottage in Kirkbride and frequented the Bush Inn, I also met many other locals who, and still are, good friends, Lenny was a good conversationalist with a great sense of humour and we would often chat away for ages about many subjects, including the local area and some of its buildings, industrial places in Carlisle, engineering, travel and a host more subjects of which Lennie was most well informed, we also spent many times joking and laughing together.

Sorry to interrupt, I've just re-read the first line, please allow me to say, I don't regard myself as a writer I prefer to say I'm a scribbler, I've always loved the written word, my grandfather kept a diary and it inspired me, books, letters, stories, a bit of verse, a post card to a friend, a scribbled note on a scrap of paper, a note on the inside cover of a book, my travel journals, and also my fishing journals, there all precious to me, it's there, recorded to visit any time, I'm not struggling in the fog of time grasping to think about a time passed, its written, yes possibly full of mistakes, but none the less there, so, as in my other scribblings this book may well contain many errors in many forms and could irritate retired English teachers, my intention is to share the adventure, the events, the humour, and the randomness, so skip the mistakes and join me.

One of my fondest memories of Lennie and me enjoying the crack was one evening I went into The Bush and Lennie was in the company of a friend of his and also the afore mentioned Ricky Turnbull, I got myself a pint and joined the company, well we were all chatting away and then Lennies friend says to Rick, "where abouts exactly in Ireland do you come from?" Rick then cocks his head to one side looks up at the fellow and says in his wonderful accent "Fuckin Haltwhistle" and then launches in to a large portion of his infectious laughter accompanied by Lennie and myself, but not so much his friend, god it was hilarious! I've often told this tale over the years and it always raises a laugh.

Lennie had been poorly and asked me if I could lend him a couple of books to read, I rattled of a few titles and then suggested a couple of my travel journals, especially the recent one of my hitch-hiking trip for Jonny, Lennie agreed and I duly dropped off the book at his house in Anthorn, he rang a week or so later and asked if we were going to meet for a pint to which I said yes, sure, when Lennie arrived at the office he put the book on the bar and said "What a laugh, that's helped me to get better, you should get it published" and from this comment, it began, so I would like to dedicate the birth of this project to Lennie.

Foreword by Jan and Dave, Jonny's parents

Young Jonny

Despite his setback Jonny was determined to live life to the full. Whether it was cooking or gardening, photography or fishing he threw himself wholeheartedly into his hobbies and gave his varied interests his all. For this and for his fighting, indomitable spirit he became a legend in his local community.

Those who came in contact with him grew to respect and admire his enthusiastic vitality. His zeal for living became contagious. It infected his growing circle of friends and often inspired them to tackle unthought of feats, to face new challenges head on. In the way Jonny would.

Peter Anderson was one of these friends. One morning Peter stepped out on a sponsored adventure to raise money for Jonny. This book is an account of his adventures and is dedicated to his friend Jonny. For this and much more we give Peter Anderson our heartfelt thanks. Dave and Jan Milne

This is my story of a hitch-hiking adventure I embarked on, from outside my local pub,   " The Kings Arms " at Bowness on Solway, in Cumbria, to Bar Miami in Mahon, Menorca,

So here goes......................................Well, The tale begins with Jonathon or Jonny as he is called, I call him Agent G, but that's another story.

Jonny is the youngest of three sons, first Columbus, or Christopher as he is known, then Steven (my left-handed engineering friend) and then Jonathan, the youngest, belonging to David and Jan, who, along with Dave and Margaret,(Jan's parents) own and run the village pub, or the office as I sometimes call it. (I miss those hot pots you used to make on a Monday night Margaret) A typical village pub in Cumbria, frequented by all sorts of individuals, My preferred time is known as early doors, when there's a regular gathering of a few of the locals, including Peter, (Editor) Bob, retired road haulage contractor, Mike, most famous for interrupting and altering conversations,

a brace of Mark Graham's, Ric the spark, Jonny the eyebrows Hogg, his brother Mike, George the bread, George the pipe, Ernie (Oliver reed look-alike and bad tempered git!) Ricky and Linda, Ricky who speaks a mixture of Irish with a smattering of Haltwhistle dialect as previously mentioned! Roger "Anyway" Brough, Ian and Hazel, good old Brian Batey, and Andrew Birkett, or as I call him, Keith Chegwin, our very own celebrity look-alike! Only he's opened more beers than supermarkets! And as previously mentioned, Dave birthday cake neck Milne, Jonny's dad.

There's nothing better on a cold winters evening than calling at home to get the fire roaring up the chimney, then a trip down to the office to put the world to rights and enjoy a good crack, boy did we all laugh, we had some great nights, and regardless of the age difference Jonny was up there with the best of them when it came to telling a tale, as well as delivering the one liners, he put many a middle aged man in his place, eh Mike? Another of Jonny's great talents were his memory, he would recall times and places in previously told stories that most of us had forgot, he could remind me of people in countries and places id long forgot and with his descriptive detail " hey Peter, remember when you were walking along the street in Mahon and a bloke from south America called Miguel shouted on you from the scaffolding, and he said you had met him when he was a waiter and a fan of Tom Jones, then you sent him some tapes and a book, then when you went back on another trip you went to see him and he said "Tonight the hotel pays for the beer" and that my dear readers is only one snippet of Jonny's ability in the memory department!

In fact it's often mentioned by the many people who are starting or finishing the Hadrian's Wall walk, how friendly and welcoming the place is. So.....without beginning to sound like I work for the tourist information board, let's get going!

Jonny has been really poorly, and in hospital in Newcastle on many occasions and many local people have raised money for the hospital in many ways, one of those was a karaoke evening, along with some of the locals who had their heads shaved! And I just don't have the nerve to sing in public so, me having slightly eccentric tendencies at times, I thought what could I do? Well, as I like Minorca, and I was planning another visit, I thought why not hitch hike! And that's how it came about. Plus, Jonny has an interest in chickens and other animals so why not raise some money for Jonny himself to spend on his hobby.

I didn't spend a lot of time planning the trip, as there was very little to plan for, as hitch-hiking is more by chance and good luck than anything else, plus my thoughts were full of daydreaming about the trip and less focused on the practical side. I was sure that if I had some basic stuff in my haversack there was little else I could do, and the rest was left to fate.

Reflecting on my past, I have had a passion for travel, solitude, and adventure for as long as I can remember, one of my first expeditions as a lad, earned me a "cuff round the listener" from my grandfather, also known as a clip round the ear! As I had sawn through a perfectly good wooden ladder to make myself a sledge for my forthcoming trip to spend a night alone on the local moss not far from the village of Creca near Annan where my grandparents had retired to, I spent many happy times with my grandparents, both hard working farming people, I loved them dearly.

So with my improvised sledge packed with fertiliser bags to make a tent, branches to support it, plenty of baling twine, (string) and a generous amount of life sustaining rock buns, off I set, complete with matches and a flash light to ward off any bears, wolves and other non-existent wild beasts. I remember pulling my sledge across the fields and setting up camp, constructing my home made tent and lying in the soft green moss and heather, slowly munching my way through the entire supply off rock buns within a short space of time. I wandered round the thin copse of woods and saw myself free, away from everything and everyone, this is the life, listening to the sounds of nature, birds, water trickling along a beck, and the odd sheep,and me with my shelter built and enjoying my little world, When darkness came it threw a different perspective on the trip, eerie sounds echoed in the night which only added to the sense of isolation, and non-existent danger of being attacked by beasts that lived in my imagination and not actually on the moss. The soft yellow glow of the back kitchen light was a comforting sight as I arrived back at my grandparent's house.

The day had finally arrived!

Got up around eight, and sat with a cup of tea, my mind wandering all over the place,

I started to pack all the stuff I had ready, into my mobile coal bunker, AKA, my haversack. Well the day had finally arrived for me to embark on my long awaited adventure, I could feel the excitement building up inside me, and couldn't wait to hit the road, I glanced around at all the things I would be taking, passport, snorkelling gear, camera, stereo, tent, sleeping bag, and a few clothes. I was taken up to the pub by my son Joe and his mum Tracey, I was going to miss them both, who, incidentally were going to Barcelona for a few days in the not too distant future with Mark, so we made arrangements to meet up there. Although the pub was closed, I was welcomed in and had a pint on the house from father Dave as we call him, Jan's Dad, we chatted for a while before getting some pictures of me and Jonny with the sign I had specially made for the trip, (cheers Craig from System signs) Also, I was given a T-shirt by Jonny which was stencilled "Peter pan" so I suggested that I would get people to sign it along the way. Soon it was time to go outside and say my goodbyes, and before long, it was time to take my first steps on my long awaited journey! So off I went, I didn't anticipate the size of the lump in my throat as I shook hands with everyone, and it was cricket ball size!

I mean it's not every day you get a free pint of Father Dave!

I wasn't a mile outside the village before I got my first lift, and it happened to be off a chap I met some years ago off the local caravan park called Brian,(who used to get me alloy off-cuts to make fuel tanks for grass track racing cars,) and his mate Tony, who took me into Carlisle, it was nice to catch up with Brian as we had often spent time chatting in the office about a great variety of subjects, they were amazed and amused at my quest.

They both wished me all the best, and we parted company outside Carr's biscuit factory in Caldewgate, where I began to contemplate my next move, when I received a text message from a lad I knew called John who asked if today was the day I was setting of on my travels, yes I replied, and asked why? Only to be told he was going to visit some friends in Liverpool and would I like a lift?

My luck was in, not only did John take me to Liverpool, but beforehand, took me to a bistro in Carlisle and bought me a meal, and got me a nights accommodation with some friends of his called Jules and Michelle when we got to Liverpool. It was hard to keep track of the conversation as we sped down the M6, as I was preoccupied with what lay ahead, and spent a lot of the time smiling and daydreaming. Jules is originally from, Wiltshire, and az a bit of an accent he does, so it wasn't long before the cider was out and we were doing some pretty crazy OoooooArgh...... type noises and impressions, and all three of us howling with laughter!

What nice people, and soon I was tucked up in a camp bed in the front room, all cosy and apple flavoured! Night night.

Woke up about 7, in the most comfortable camp bed ie ever slept in, and lay there thinking about the day ahead, who would I meet today I wonder? And where would I end up tonight?

So, after lashings of wonderful ideas in my head, I wrenched myself from the camp bed, got shaved and showered, made a cup of tea, and here I am, so to speak, I think Michelle said last night, her mum may be able to give me a lift to the motorway, spent an hour or so chatting to Jules and Michelle,(her mum is still in bed, so no lift) and then hit the road, they walked me up to the main road and we said our goodbyes, not before I asked" is that the docks" yeah, Jules said, so I am now contemplating going to one of the shipping company's to see if I can get a boat ride! Where to I do not know! Now in a greasy spoon type of café, with the mobile coal-bunker taking up a lot of space, I never realised how many things I was going to knock over, or bang into in the coming days! Looking for a dock worker, I spoke to a couple of chaps and explained my bright idea of scrounging a lift on a ship, they told me I may be better of going to the shipping office.

Just finished breakfast, and now I'll go and have a chat with the people at the shipping office, just had two lifts, first of a tipper driver from Birkenhead to Liverpool, a real easy going sort of a chap. And the second was with a really dodgy fellow who was kind enough to drive me all-round the docks, needless to say I didn't ask him many questions!

And soon I was in a huge traffic office, and joined the queue, only to be told I couldn't just walk along the wharf and chat to crews and bum a ride on a ship. but, they did give me a phone number of a shipping company, who go to Bilbao, got contact number of a chap called Paul Mac, real decent egg, who said the ship to Bilbao had sailed today! I was disappointed to say the least, Oh god, what a lift that would have been! My mind went into overdrive, imagine offering to work and ending up with a boiler suit on and down in the engine room, home of a massive lump of an engine and getting to help out, so with a slightly heavy heart I set off for a look around the docks, it was really hot and the haversack seemed to get heavier with every step! There were ships coming and going to and from all sorts of places, which helped lift my spirits and reminded me of the coming random events that would twist and turn to form my destiny on the voyage, this added to my sense of excitement and adventure. and soon after having a word with myself I was back on top form, spent some time just wallowing in the solitude of my situation, it was as if I was isolated from the everyday toil of life itself, even though it was only to be for a week or two.

I then got a lift of a real quiet chap to a place called Fisher gate, which is near Wigan, so I appear to be going in the wrong direction, oh shit! So I am now standing on a roundabout thumb sticking out at each vehicle. Sometime later..... Been here for five and a half hours, and virtually melting, and not a glimmer of hope on the lift front, it was then I decided to have a nap, so I lay down in the grass and was soon fast asleep, sometime later I awoke to find a chap in a high-viz jacket holding what appeared to be a metal bar leaning over me, I was slightly shocked at this as he asked me what I was doing to which I replied "having a rest, what are you doing?" I felt a lot more at ease when he told me he worked for the water board and was looking for a drain! We chatted briefly and he was amused at my explanation, so after a brief chat I get the coal-bunker on my back, and set off down the road towards a village, and low and behold I come across a pub, so I decide to go in for a cool pint of lager, and plan my next move, I don't know whether to go back on the road again, or look for somewhere to sleep for the night, will decide soon, having said that, now that I'm sitting with a cool pint in front of me I don't feel much like doing any more walking today, sometime later............. I call into another pub,(looking for B+B, of course) and got talking, (not like me I hear some of you say!) to a couple of joiners Dale and Martin who noticed my sign that I had laid on the bar and began to ask what I was doing and where I was going, they were really friendly and helpful, they were from T.M.C. Joiners and shop fitters Ltd, At first, they could not believe that I was on such a trip, hitching to Minorca, and soon I earned the name "the crazy teacher!" Anyway, after getting chatting to them and other locals, they recommend I perhaps stay at the Swan, and catch up with them later in another pub called "The last orders" as there was a Soul night on, and me being into said music I agreed,(should be fun, let's see!) The Swan is an old railway hotel, with etched glass windows, and ornate doors. cheap accommodation and only a few miles down the road, so, after a couple more pints off I set in a taxi with one of the locals, who would not hear of me paying towards the journey, and got duly dropped off at the place.

It was run by a mother and daughter team, who were very friendly and were amused at my tale of such a journey to hitch to Minorca.

I dumped the coal-bunker, and while lying on the bed, began to look out of the window at some of the marvellous buildings that surrounded the place, some of the brickwork is brilliant and the chimneys fantastic, the evening sun added to the beauty of the brickwork as it warmed it up, Fred Dibner came to mind as I had once watched a program of his early years and he had built a very ornate chimney on his mams terraced home, I do like a bit of Fred's type of stuff, old buildings, chimneys, steam contraptions, and various other old world topics he has featured on his series, anyway, I then had a shower and got some very creased clothes out of the coal bunker.

So, looking like I was on my way to an ironing competition, off I set down the main street looking for the afore mentioned pub, and Lancashire people being the friendly sort, I was soon armed with directions.
 When I turned up Dale and Martin were pleased to see me, it was a great place bouncing with great soul and jazz funk music, Oh man, this is gonna be great I thought,
they must have mentioned the crazy teacher, and introduced me to countless people, I have never shook hands with so many people in the one night who kept handing me fiver's galore! And due to the excellent sounds and large portions of delicious lager, it wasn't

long before I was on the floor, dancing I mean, not drunk! It was great and I was buzzing, everyone dancing, laughing, and generally enjoying themselves.

At one stage I was in the company of a Scandinavian female solicitor, no! Not that type!!!! I mean the legal profession! who was very attractive indeed, as well as a good dancer and conversationalist, we must have had six or seven dances, which we both enjoyed, yum yum! And, had some good chats about many subjects.

Newsflash! Text from Jen.

As the soul night was in a Pub, the jollifications came to an end at around midnight and Dale and Martin insisted I go clubbing with them, their friends, and the girls. After a quick drunken risk assessment mainly fuelled by thoughts of staggering around a strange town centre with a kebab and a head like a toy shop I decided I must be a good boy, go back to the Swan and get good night's sleep so I was reasonably fresh for the next day's adventure, but before I left they wished me well and all gave me some more sponsor money for Jonny, what kind people, I was touched by their generosity.

I am now sitting in the dining room of the swan and station, waiting for my breakfast, I reflect on last night, boy it was some do, just meeting them lads in a random pub and due to them being them it was a micro adventure in the main picture so to speak, I was really enjoying the randomness of the trip and it tickled me, and while I scribbled in my travel journal, I got talking to a chap called Harry, who works as a guard on the railway. A real decent sort of a chap who told me briefly about his work and the travelling he does as part of it.

As he asked me what I was doing here, I began to tell him the tale of my adventure, and as I had a sudden idea to hitch a lift on a train, I ran it past him. He said it is well worth a try and perhaps I may do best if I go and have a word with the stationmaster. (Sounds like something from the railway children)

Also in the dining room was a really nice lady called Mildred, who came from Yorkshire and was visiting relatives here in Wigan, as she was a lone traveller I felt it best not to ask too many questions, yet soon, all three of us were chatting away.

Just finished breakfast, and due to being on tour, and lots of walking not to mention the weight of the coal-bunker (AKA rucksack) I have decided to eat each morning to keep the energy levels topped up, I don't usually eat in the morning but this is a serious mission!

Been to the local shops to get all IT, problems sorted, camera is charged and working, and the stereo does go really loud! And that's vital.

So, meanwhile I am sitting in a café writing cards to folks back at home, and a progress up-date to the kings arms in Bowness, plus a text to Jen, so now I will go and collect my kit and get back on the road again.

Sometime later, I'm sitting in another café at the station, I have spoken to a nice girl by the name of Tina who is a team leader about getting a free ride on a train south. She is very helpful and suggested I speak to the train manager, and she informs me there is a train due in shortly going to Birmingham, if I can manage to get a lift on that, it would be super de duper to say the least!

And guess who is on said train? Yes it's me, Peter Pan, I took Tina's advice and spoke to Bob, the train manager outlining my adventure and with no hesitation whatsoever he said to me "you've literally got 10 seconds to get on the train" so I am now going as far as Birmingham for free! Good old Bob eh? (The train changes there, so it's all dependant on my begging skills to determine whether I get to Penzance) with Bobs help with the negotiations as we stood on the platform all went well at Birmingham, and now on another train, yippee!

This certainly beats standing on the roadside melting for hours! Now sitting at a table writing, and occasionally gazing out of the window, heading south towards the channel and devising a plan to cross it for free. But me being me, I already have one or two cunning plans up my sleeve as Baldric would say.
I am literally buzzing at the thought of being near some water tonight, music, a few lagers, writing, music, and solitude.

The track is running alongside the sea, it's great! warm and sunny, with sailing boats, speedboats, and rowing boats, all living in harmony, as the country side slowly passes it is ideal for just gazing out of the windows and letting my thoughts go into free-fall.

We are getting near to Plymouth as people are beginning to gather their stuff together, not long been off the train and now loafing around beside the water, Ahh bliss! Just had a phone call of Mike Miller, the afore mentioned champion interrupter! from the village, lucky bar steward is in Paris for a Rolling Stones concert! Hey, I was just thinking, I bet he doesn't interrupt "Mick Jagger" mind you!!!!!

Had a wander around Plymouth, and now heading towards a hostel, meanwhile I have called into a pub called the walrus and met some more people, Hey this is some place ie had myself a couple of pints and met Barry (Canadian) and Wendy, a real nice couple. Then came across two older type chaps who just happen to be coming out of one of the local pubs, looking like something from the last of summer wine! So I can't resist going over to chat to them. and me being me, I decide to record the event by telling them I need some help, and if I switch on the short video function on the camera could they say hello to Jonny, so whilst trying my best to suppress my laughter, I say 3-2-1 ready, and in a really funny west country accent they say "hello Jonny" I was Fuckin crying man, and the more I laughed the more they did! I couldn't stop myself, oh god!

Also met two women whose names I can't remember, and some big-headed bloke from London, so I listened to his nonsense before heading to said hostel only to find it is full! But the chap says "go next door and see Tony" who turns out to be a Chinese chap.

Well, when I was in reception a French girl came in, wanting her cycle to be put in the hall, and because of all the rucksacks and the fact we sort of arrived together, the Chinese chap thinks I am with her, and suggests we bunk up together! Talk about laugh, Chinese, English, and French, all trying to explain at the same time! It was hilarious to say the least!

So, confusion over, I had a shower and sorted out my kit, and put some nice tunes on the stereo, and soon was fast asleep, what a marvellous day.

" Last breakfast " was the shout at the door, it was Tony the Chinese chap, and when I came down and into the dining room it was mostly full with a group of Welsh blokes on a diving holiday.

Tony then showed me to a table for two, and already sitting there was the French girl Sonria! I think Tony has some hidden urge to play matchmaker, so I sit down and we eat breakfast together and chat about various things, she is very interesting and works as an architect, and is looking forward to cycling around the south coast.

Sometime later….. been loafing around Plymouth, very nice place and lots of really friendly type people all willing to help with anything. Now in a café writing my journal

along with postcards to various people including an up-
date to the king Arms pub. Another text to and from Jen,
it's great to have her support along the way.

The digital camera seems to be taking the day off, and
I'm getting really frustrated with it, I swear at it like were a
couple having a row on holiday, smiling to those around
like were the picture of happiness, and between gritted
and crunching teeth say things in a cutting sarcastic way
like "that's really Fuckin handy you spoiling things" only
to get a reply like "you complete shit I should never have
come away with you, the girls were right" so I called into
a camera shop to get some advice and download what's
on it to a disc in case I lose the lot, only to be told by the
IT master behind the counter that there was loads more
room on the card for lots and lots of nice pictures, I
insisted he put them on a CD anticipating me and the
cameras turbulent relationship while he explains it's like
two or three beans in a tin, I smile and keep on acting
like the thick individual he thinks I am. He gets 99p I get
a mostly empty CD and I'm happy.
Called into a few shops, including some charity ones,
also a good bookshop and saw a fantastic book about
classic tractors, so ie bought it and sent it to Hoggy a lad
called Mike Hogg from home (Poor buggers been gay
badly thoo noz) Also bought some pencils and a glue
stick for stuff going into the travel journal, receipts etc.,
and some rough drawings, and I am really enjoying all
the writing and scribbling and my attempts at drawing.
And, just as important, recording the events as they
happen with lashings of good crack to share with Jonny.

After my wander around the shops I went back for the coal-bunker and walked all the way to the ferry terminal only to find the ferry is fully booked for the next crossing. And then it began to rain, and it is still raining so I decided to go back to the hostel to find that is full too! And am I concerned? No, not at all, been to buy a brolly so I'm sorted, legs still working and I'm dry so why worry? " I'm walking in the rain, just walking in the rain " I am going to hitch to Portsmouth tomorrow and see if I can hitch a ride on a boat," Adventure is for the Adventurous " (read that some years ago, somewhere, and never forgot it, could be Will shaky spear). For health reasons, I decide instead of aimlessly wandering about in the rain I may sample the local lager and end up in the appropriately named bar Walkabout and get chatting to the bar-person called Cos. He's a sort of surf type dude, and
very interesting regarding the local area, so we spend some time chatting about various subjects, work, money, girls, and life in general. Moments later I am joined at the bar by an Australian chap whose name I can't remember due to the amount of alcohol that we are both consuming, he is a bit of a character to say the least! And things are getting madder by the minute, we carry on drinking for a while then soon tire of each other's company and I decide to move on, wishing him all the best while trying to sound sincere.

Outside it is absolutely pouring down, so I take shelter in another pub, I must not go on the lash I say to myself, with the conviction of a politician!

Not long after, I get talking to some welsh chap at the bar called Keith, who has a big tummy and an even bigger heart, as he gives me ten pounds sponsor money for Jonny, he is with his mates called Nicolas and Steve, (Steve has scribbled in the travel journal a few words, says I'm a great bloke, how kind) and there are lashings of good crack, and even bigger lashings of ale flowing, SESSION IMMINENT! And then, another chap called Paul from Liverpool joins us and we are having a hilarious time laughing and joking, they too think my hitch-hiking trip is not only slightly odd, but also amazing as talk about Jonny and explain it to them. We spend a long time enjoying each other's company and the time slips by like no-one is too concerned about it, and all of a sudden it is night. So I decide I'm in no fit state to present myself at the door of the hostel. so hoist the coal-bunker onto my back with some assistance from the lads, and after lots of good hearty handshakes and well wishes I wander off in a zigzag fashion, heading out of town with some ill thought out idea that I will put the tent up for the night. And what a silly thought it was! I ended up sleeping in a field, only to wake up the next day and momentarily think the tent had been pinched while I was asleep! TRAVEL TIP! Always put the tent up before going to the pub!

Hi there, so glad to be back! Just had an early morning major self-induced IT breakdown, as in I fiddled with some of the settings on the camera and it went into a sort of I'm not playing any more mode, in fact ie actually got to own up, I have done it a few times lately. It may be time for me to repair our relationship! The camera screen goes all black and white and starts to run through all the settings and then it kinda stops, and asks questions. And I always click on yes (naively thinking I'm keeping the thing happy) thank goodness I don't work in the nuclear industry!   so….. back to the tale.

anyway, its morning and with a slight hangover I manage to find a bottle of water in the bag to quench my raging thirst, brush my teeth, and sort of get a very basic wash and reflect on the previous evening. Then after being on the roadside for a little while I get a lift of Phil, a van driver, and generally chatted about nothing in particular, some lifts are like that, not much to say, and others like a canary convention! Chirping away like there's no tomorrow. So now, I am in Portsmouth walking around the town centre and generally daydreaming, and enjoying the often-felt feeling of not being bothered about anything in particular.

Due to my interest in boats I head down to the harbour for two reasons, firstly to look at the boats, and secondly to see if I can manage to scrounge a lift across the channel. After strolling around for a while I come across a fishing boat registered in Dumfries and got talking to the skipper and some of the crew, and at one stage I heard this distinctive voice, and I say are you from west Cumberland? To which the chap replies yis marra, where's thou frae? When I tell him Bowness on Solway near Wigton he is amazed! So we have a good old crack about home and various other subjects. He is a real smashing bloke, by the name of Rob.

I also spent a bit of time talking to the skipper, who informed me that they had to chase the fish to make money, and they were heading for the Scilly isles, and I knew it was a little off route so to speak, but I just couldn't help but blurt out, hey! That will do! the chance to go somewhere else along the trip just appealed to me so much, I couldn't resist. The skipper also told me they may be other boats in the isles that were going to other places, France included, and this only reinforced my adventurous impulsiveness!

I sat down on the boat and began to wonder whom I would meet next, and the thought of getting off onto the Scilly isles, and the next leg of the journey, would it be a fishing boat? A small freighter? Or perhaps a beautiful yacht!

While they are getting ready to go to sea, they find that one of the derricks (that's a crane to you and me) is seized up, so they have to change the pulley wheel. And the next thing, I'm up to the elbows in grease and getting stuck in with them, with sparks flying from the grinder, and the oxyacetylene gear, in all. I would say we were at it for about 4-5 hours, first the giant nut holding in the pin was jammed solid, next thing the stillsons (big wrench) broke, so after going to another boat a little further up the quay. We managed to borrow another big wrench and after lots of wrestling with the split pin, lashings of treatment with the acetylene torch we managed to get the nut loose a little, it seemed to take forever to get it to the last few threads! We were all sweating a bit due to a combination of a lovely warm sunny day, and the ferocious heat from the mixture of acetylene and oxygen, that came from the torch.

After our mammoth bout with the large nut, we sat around talking and drinking tea, and I spoke to Rob about Workington, and generally about Cumberland, as well as other things in life, family, girlfriends, work, and some of the crew members, including a Chinese fellow who couldn't speak a word of English, and the poor blighters name? China! Trust the crew to call him that! Having said that, it was a howl watching them communicate, shouting for pliers, cup of tea, spanners etc, it was all I could do, not to burst out laughing at times, but they too were laughing at some of the crack, and equally important, so was China himself!

The skipper then began to get ready to go to sea, and part of the process was to monitor the radio for weather and fishing reports, imagine my disappointment when he told me they would not be going to the Scilly isles but straight out of harbour and into the channel, to chase the fish, I was so cheesed off! The thought of a bottle of champagne soon helped me get over this slight setback!

On route I came across a wine shop, and it wasn't long before I had said bottle of champagne about my persons and headed back down to the Quayside to see the chaps off. I shook hands with them all, and wished them luck, paying particular attention to Rob, shared some of the bottle with them and watched as the boat slowly crept out of the harbour against a beautiful red sky. How I wished I were going with them.

Deciding to enjoy the gorgeous sunset and what was left of the champagne, I got myself parked up on the quayside and put on some lovely Sade (pronounced sharday) tunes. I don't recall exactly how long I sat there, but the ambience of it was awesome. So tranquil and thought provoking, sweet soulful music, the sky now a flaming mixture of red and orange, to a solo traveller this was heaven! I remember sitting there until the sun had long gone, and around the harbour, the lights reflected off the water. In fact I didn't want to leave, it was such a feeling.

After I don't know how long, I decided to go for a wander along the harbour side, not realising the champagne had began to have an effect on me and my legs! I saw a bar and decided in my wisdom to pop in. As I stood at the bar scribbling in my travel journal I became aware of one or two people stealing glances at me, swaying gently in my flip-flops, shorts, an T-shirt with a nearly empty bottle at my feet, and me smirking to myself, so happy and so carefree!
I have heard the saying "don't mix the grape with the grain" and wow! The alcohol mixture was really starting to get to me, but I was so much enjoying myself I really didn't care at this stage of the proceedings. And had a couple of pints before I started to play Find the coal bunker, which I had hidden on the harbour, I was swimming in a mixture of champagne, lager, and the

euphoria of being so free, I got parked up on the harbour and put on more music and rolled out my sleeping bag before laying back and drifting off into a deep sleep.

Woke up the next morning felling like I had been knocking about with the rolling stones, so after scraping the fur of my tongue with my toothbrush, and getting a basic bottle wash, I'm ready to hit the road again. May head for Exeter, but first, I must eat. So I am now safely parked up in a small café eating a Cornish pasty with gravy, so I am my dears! And it tastes really yummy. And while I scribble away at my journal the photos and video clips I have taken are in a photo shop being transferred onto a disc. Sometimes the digital stuff and all the technology twists my melon! Good job I don't work in a place where there's loads of buttons to press! Could be disastrous.

Been back to the photo shop to collect the c.d. and as luck had it, they have Internet access so ie sent a few e-mails to peoples, including Jen. Now having a cup of tea on the pavement, at a table of course, outside a cafe not actually sitting on the pavement. And I continue to attract the odd glance from people. On reflection, with a rucksack the size of a coal-bunker, the constant writing and colouring in of my small drawings, I could be perceived as a little odd. Don't answer that!

I must remember to delete some texts, as there are loads, I haven't really been giving much thought to the phone the last day or two, or to the date or what day it actually is, which only increases my sense of freedom, and lack of care.

Now parked up outside another pub, having only one pint (honest), just met Steve, Clare, and their kids, real nice people. Steve is into soul music and in particular, a great George Benson fan, we compare notes on singles, albums and memories we both have of the great soul artist along with the likes of bobby Wommack, Luther Vandross, and many others, so we get along fine.

I am feeling a little tired, so I may take a nap, but I must remember to get a snack for later on tonight, a sarnie or something, I'm now going to finish writing even more postcards that I have bought up town.

Just met Ben and Brian, a father and son from Glasgow, doing some contract work here, they are really nice blokes. And they too give me some sponsor money.

Sometime later………. I've walked about six miles, bag comfortable, yet heavy. Now having lunch, which is beans on fried bread. Then back on the road again, I'm very tempted to go to north Cornwall and try a bit of surfing, or do I head south towards the coast again? I do tend to get distracted at times, as you have no doubt gathered!

Made my way to Exeter, by way of a couple of lifts, people are a bit amused when I ask them to sign the t-shirt that Jonny gave me. Spent some time wandering around and looking at some of the fantastic buildings.

Exeter must be the worst place on earth for people knocking into my rucksack! Especially as it's not exactly small, and can't be seen.

Just been to the bus company to ask for a free lift to help me on my journey, but all I got was funny looks and a few sniggers of the drivers! Most of them overweight, eating like pigs, and some of them a little sweaty! They looked like they were at a friar tuck convention! I did explain the reason for my hitch-hiking trip, to raise some sponsor money for Jonny. But they looked at me like I was a complete misfit. So me being me, I decided to tell them what I thought, it went like this, "Hey, that's cool if you don't want to help, your all fat, and stuck here, I'm not, and I'm leaving, see ya " he who laughs last laughs loudest!

I wandered off and down an underpass and got some great photos of the graffiti on the walls while still smirking about the friar, tuck club!

Feeling on top hiking form, I walked out of town and into the open country side for some miles, and it began to rain, but I kept going, it rained for about two hours before I eventually got a lift of a chap named James who informs me during our conversation that he is doing a PHD. in marine biology, and similar to me, he loves snorkelling, and told me some good places for in the morning. So here I am in Torquay! Now in a Caribbean style bar, it's really good, met Pete, who owns the place with his dad, really cool inside, the décor, palms, flags, painted white shutters, plants, and some funky reggae music, also met Chris, who works for a housing company, and is originally from Edinburgh, a nice chap.

Just been to Tesco for a snack for later, (lovely salad) and having a couple of pints before an early night, see ya later.

And now is later, me lying on the bed in a really old fashioned type B+B that I came across, run by a chap called Brian, who reminds me of the little bloke from a TV programme called "it aint half hot mum "ie put some nice music on (Lisa Stansfield) and now busy eating chicken and pasta salad, with a bottle of Spanish beer, Es bien si? (is ok yes) it's bloody great! Let me tell you, I may turn into a professional hitch-hiker! TRAVEL TIP, if there's no drinks fridge in the supermarket, hide the beer/champagne in amongst the frozen veg, go for a wander, return, get the rest of your stuff and pick up your chilled drinks!

Before going to bed, I went to the bathroom and discovered a huge bath that could quite easily get me across the channel! So I fill it to the brim and immerse myself in the lovely hot water, it was heaven! And, after I don't know how long I go to bed, and very soon fall fast asleep.

Got up around 6. 30. Washed and shaved, just about packed the rucksack, and nearly ready for the off. Now sitting at a table in the dining room waiting for breakfast, this really is an old fashioned place, with a floral standard lamp, ancient wallpaper, and a large bookcase along one wall. Yet it is really cozy and friendly. I think I will nip upstairs and finish packing, and then go for a wander along the sea front and perhaps find a cyber café to send some e-mails.

Been along the sea front and went to some of the places that James recommended to snorkel, it was great, the water nice and clear, and not at all cold, yet again I'm enjoying the freedom of just floating around in the water and watching the fish as they scurry for cover among the rocks and plants. It's almost like a world within a world, the complete freedom of the trip itself and extended even further by the detachment of not being connected to anything, land, people, or any sounds at all. I float around for ages, got out dried and changed, Then shortly after the skies darkened, and a cloudburst, with the rain bouncing off the pavement, so I decide to take shelter in a café, do some writing, send some postcards, and spend a little time daydreaming while looking over the harbour. A very moody scene, so romantic.

Sometime later…….after walking for ages with heavy rucksack I got a lift with a chap in a small wagon, to Portsmouth, again he was amused at my request to sign the t-shirt for Jonny. We chatted about cars, wagons, road haulage, and many other subjects along the way. For some reason it seems to be taking ages to get to our destination. Still, at least I am making some progress. Must remember, "Beggars can't be choosers "

It's really nice to be looking out of the window, and taking in all the scenery, I feel really tired today with all the walking, but I'm loving every step of the way. And each ride I get in all the different vehicles. I am tempted to have a nap, but I feel it's a bit rude especially as the bloke has stopped to give me a lift, so when I yawn, looking like I'm auditioning for a lion bar advert, I look out of the window so that the driver can't see me.

Just sent a text to my mate Jen, but it wouldn't send as I have got no signal, so I will try later, I did try later but still no signal, so I ask our driver if he has one, no he replies, not good for signal in this area, ah well, it's not just me then. Another hour or so and I should be in Portsmouth, and hopefully ratching around the harbour, great! I love boats, in fact, boats are me.com hee hee!

At last I'm in Portsmouth, Yippee! I have spent what seems like an eternity looking for a hostel, but had no luck at all, but all is not lost as I have come across a B+B pub, and its famously named "The lady Hamilton " which is full of Nelson memorabilia and wonderful paintings, which I have taken some photos of, this will do fine!
I have just been for a walk around the waterfront, to look at some of the boats that are tied up along the quay, one of them is a real old one, with huge great wooden masts and lots and lots of sails, wooden pulleys that miles and miles of rope run through, with port holes for the canons.
I decide to sit a while and just watch the world go by, and spend some time in daydream mode, imagining myself at sea on the old ship travelling to all sorts of exotic faraway places, tales of wild adventure come to mind fuelled by

some of the many books ie read, places ie been, my constant harbour walking, and an affinity with water, After travelling across the globe in the good ship "daydream "I return to reality and head back to the lady Hamilton.

There is only a handful of people in the bar, ie just met some really great lads, Steve, Chimp, Joe, and Sam the barman (the most important) who instead of giving me sponsor money, they decide to buy me a few pints, which is really nice of them, they ask me about the trip, how it came about, the village, Bowness pub and the people, I do my best to give an accurate picture of home and life there, especially focusing on the friendships and bonds that exist, and in turn I ask them about the place, them, and their lives, (must be careful here, the lager is going down well and I'm getting urges to compliment my descriptions of characters back by doing impersonations!) and yet again the nature of my trip has them amused and amazed, as I am with the trip, sometimes the whole thing gets out of hand when my mind starts wandering, it's like being in a road movie! I'm amazed at peoples kindness and good wishes not only for me doing the trip, but more important for Jonny

I am feeling really tired, yet still well happy, and can't wait to roll into bed, but I think I may ring the pub at Bowness to give them an up-date, Its now 11.30. and I am off to bed, as I am really tired, I didn't realise how tired I would get on the trip. After giving this some thought, I realise it's all the walking with the heavy rucksack, and perhaps not eating as often as I should, must have a word with myself!

After a good night's sleep, here I am sitting in the dining room eating breakfast and scribbling in my journal, it's a beautiful day outside and the sun is shining. I feel more energetic today, so I will get my kit packed, hoist the coal-bunker onto my back, and hit the road again. But for now I am content to just sit here and relax a little, probably due to just having eaten a decent breakfast. More later……

And now, sometime later, here I am sitting in a café having a cup of tea and scribbling in my journal, as well as writing more postcards. I have just met a family who are on holiday, mum, Dad, Beth, Jordan, Tiff, and Anna Marie, had a nice chat about all sorts of things, houses, money, kids, and playing old fashioned games, before we all became obsessed with the television. I am now heading for a place called North end to ratch around the charity shops, as ie been informed there are lots of them, I'm actually on the bus across town as I write this. Had a right good time mooching around the charity shops, and bought myself a couple of C.D.s, then popped into a local bakery for a delicious ham and tomato roll in brown bread, swiftly followed by a wait of over half an hour at the wrong bus stop, and only just made the ferry. I did manage to get some discount due to my sponsored hitch hike, after first pleading for a free trip, which fell on deaf ears. So here I am on the boat crossing to Cherbourg in France. I have made a short video clip as the boat was leaving the harbour, ie done a few of them, but due to my poor I.T. skills with the digital camera I'm not that confident they will be all that good.

I am really enjoying the crossing, it's a lovely sunny evening, and I hope I got some good photos, in the lounge area there is a screen showing a sat nav type of chart, and were edging nearer to France. I can't decide whether to loaf around in Cherbourg, or just hit the road, I will probably decide when I get there. NEWSFLASH! Just had my first glimpse of France! Now writing with a French pen from the ferry staff as ie lost my good gel pen, all say Ahh.

And my dear readers, here I am in France! Yippee! After a slow walk around the harbour to look at the boats and ships, I soon spotted some trucks that had just come off another ferry so I went to speak to the drivers and ie got myself a lift all the way to Alicante in Spain, in a cattle truck, how lucky is that? (it all went wrong later)

The truck drivers name is Wem, and he is on his way back from southern Ireland, he is from Belgium and is taking his load of cows to a farm in southern Spain so it is a real good lift, he speaks about four languages, and has about the same number of mobile phones for some unknown reason. And so.... we set off on our journey winding our way south and heading for Spain, and as we travel we chat away and slowly get to know each other. Me reading the map and Wem, cursing and swearing at most of the traffic signs, as well as his tachograph which limits his driving hours, not that it seems to bother him all that much, as he later reveals he has fixed up some sort of device that fools the tachograph into not recording his driving time, or his speed! I know in the UK it is very naughty to do such things, and often brings on a guest appearance at the local magistrates court, complete with a severe thinning of the wallet! Thoughts spring to mind of spending some time in a Spanish prison for being an accomplice to such deeds!

Some of the roads are a bit dangerous to say the least, but Wem keeps his foot on the loud pedal and trucks on! Well, we are now in Nantes, about 350 kilometres from Cherbourg, and have been driving all through the night. He drives like Michael Schumacher! Wem is a good conversationalist and he asks many times to repeat my plans for the trip, which always seems to bring a smile to his lips. This is all a bit crazy yeah; we have passed Bordeaux, and have covered around 1,000 kilometres. At one stage, Wem asks me if I can drive an articulated truck? That's a massive big thing pulling a 40ft trailer, complete with beef burgers on-board! To which I answer a definite no, I have actually drove one, but to put a stop to any suicidal thoughts he may have I think it best to stick to this answer.

As the truck rumbles on and we carry on eating up the kilometres, we talk about all sorts of things, work, life, and we soon get onto the subject of girls, when Wem tells me his girlfriend is a jeweller, and goes on to tell me the turbulent tale of how they got together. Including him bashing her former boyfriend, who was treating her badly, and spending her money. Not long after this, he reveals he has to see a psychologist before going back to court in Belgium. So, I tactfully and slowly change the subject, before he launches into some sort of anger management programme! Christ! I am beginning to recall phrases like "one sandwich short of a picnic" "not the full shilling" and many other similar expressions.

I keep getting tired, and jump into the bunk bed for a nap now and then, and Wem asks me "why do you fuckin sleep so much?" I tell him I don't often do thousands of kilometres in trucks, and the motion of it sends me to sleep, which he finds funny.

Sometime later.........We are now in a French farmyard, and have just unloaded 74 cows, when a chap comes out of a shed, hands me a pitchfork, and says to me" vous avec les animals?" which I think means, are you with the cows, so I say no, I'm with this chap, and point to Wem, who briefly explains to the chap he is giving me a lift. So, after lashings of bonjour m'sieur, and hearty handshakes, I accept the pitchfork, this could only happen to me! But I'm loving every minute of it. Apparently, as we are doing a long distance, it is usual to stop on the way for the night to feed and water the cows.

I now have on a boiler suit, and wellies, and armed with said pitchfork, busy myself cleaning the muck and straw from the 40ft trailer, with help from Wem, who never ceases to curse and swear.

And what makes him swear even more is my laughter, when he says "is fuckin funny yeah" so I tell him it really is because he has collected the cows from southern Ireland and he is shouting at them in Spanish! And to make matters worse, when we are sending them down an alleyway towards a shed, one of them kicks out at me, and I fall over in fits of laughter and end up with a streak of green cow shit from my ankle to my ear! And the more he swears, the more I laugh, almost to the point of peeing myself, while at the same time crying, soon after we go to our rooms, with only me smiling.

We are soon called into the farmhouse by the farmer's wife, who has prepared us a typical French breakfast, which consists of fresh baguettes, fried ham and eggs, cheese and fruit, which is more like an evening meal! She asks Wem in French if I will speak to her as she apparently loves to hear English being spoken, so I do my best to hold a conversation with her and she seems pleased, and is slightly perplexed when she hears my tale of the journey I am on, yet amused at the same time. When we get the cattle settled,(sounds like we are putting them to bed) and have a shower we sit out in the yard with a couple of bottles of French wine, and gradually Wem begins to see the funny side of things, only to start me laughing again when he asks if I think the cows will understand Spanish. Along with asking if I think, the animals are looking all right. So doing my best to placate him, I tell him yeah there looking fit and well, then after chatting for a while we retire to our rooms, which are up in the eaves of the farmhouse.

The rooms are really quaint, with old beams, tiled floors and a window overlooking the farmyard and across the countryside, so I plonk my stuff on the floor and go for a much needed shower, and scribble away to record today's events, continually smiling at the situation I am in. Meanwhile Wem is having a chat with the farmer so I decide to go for a walk down the lane to look around and take one or two photos.

I am constantly loosing track of the time as well as the days, as we go to our rooms for a sleep the crazy bad tempered trucker Wem tells me we are loading the cows back into the truck later tonight and then hitting the road for another night drive. Along with the fact, we should be in Alicante by about 12 o'clock tomorrow, which is good news.

Once again we are called into the farmhouse to eat, and feeling like I am entering a let's get fat competition we sit down to soup with French bread, steak and chips, yoghurt, then fruit, and of course a bottle of wine, god I'm stuffed!

After a little time chatting, we re-load the truck with much swearing and cursing from Wem, and soon we are back on the road, a couple of times the brakes don't seem to work on the trailer, and this makes him madder than ever. So we stop a few times to check the airlines that take the air from the truck to the trailers brakes, Sometime later......... we are now just outside Madrid, and have covered over seven hundred kilometres in about seven hours. We then stop at a petrol station as Wem is going to have a nap for half an hour, I'm beginning to have my doubts about this chap.

Not long after he wakes up and soon we are trucking along, he mentions the brakes again, and infers that it's my fault! We have a row about his cursing and swearing, so I can't help myself and proceed to tell him that his attitude needs adjusting, which he doesn't like at all. So, after a bit of a stony silence, he apologises and says that he is a bit stressed out, not only with the cows, but also with life in general. Then goes on to mention that he is worried about having to see the psychologist before going back to court. I then get thoughts like bale out! Exit!

After much checking of the map and re-checking, we get nearer to the farm we are going to deliver the cows to, we call into a roadside café and order some snacks, while Wem checks we are going in the right direction by showing the place on the map to some Spanish truck drivers. The place is really busy with lots of drivers ordering food in rapid Spanish, and the waitress speaking back with equal speed. He is good at speaking Spanish, as well as French, a little German, and god knows what other languages. A few kilometres later and we pull off the main road and wind our way along a dusty track, and eventually come to the farm, which covers a large area with literally hundreds of cattle in massive fields that are mostly dust. The sun is really hot and with some of the cattle, we bake.

Most of the fields have steel structures, which are in fact sunshades for the cattle to escape the heat of the sun, there basically four steel girders with tin roofs. The owner comes up to the truck to meet us and speaks mostly to Wem, as my Spanish is confined to hola, bon dias, which means hello, good day. He then shows us which shed he wants them in and we back the truck up to it and proceed to un-load the cows. The owner of the farm and his brother look carefully at them as they clatter down the aluminium tailgate, checking they are not cut, bruised, or otherwise damaged. They then get out the paperwork and Wem gets the necessary signatures.

Meanwhile, we drive the truck over to a large heap of straw and shit, and add to it the contents of the trailer, and the heat along with the stench of the urine is overpowering at times. So much in fact, that every now and then we have to get out of the trailer for some fresh air. Wem tells me that on one trip it was so bad, the ammonia caused him to faint in the back of the trailer, I was tempted to have a snigger at this, but not wishing to bring on another bout of cursing I decide to stifle it. After much heaving with forks and shovels, the trailer is emptied, the heat inside was unbelievable, we were both sweating loads and wearing boiler suits only added to this.

Soon after we were back on the road again and heading south, Wem said he had a load of tiles to collect in Alicante and the trailer must be washed out before he can get re-loaded. I asked how we were going to do that and he told me we would go to a garage with a pressure washer, which, after some time we found.

I went into the garage and was told the machine took Euros, and as wem had given me 30 Euros in notes, I changed it into coins for the machine. I then put 10 of them into the machine and we started to wash out the trailer, but soon after the machine stopped! Well he went mad, cursing and swearing like a man possessed! I went back into the garage and explained that something was wrong with the machine as it had gobbled up all the Euros and shortly stopped. Only to be told there was a timer on it, and the coins had to be put in one at a time, well you can imagine how Wem reacted when I told him! Boy was he mad! I also was beginning to get a little annoyed at his constant swearing, which he seemed to be directing at me.

So we then put them in as advised, one at a time, which only added to his frustration and fury! Along with having to pass the hose up and down the trailer through the gaps in the bars so we could go from one end to the other. It was when he got the hose stuck that the final eruption came, and this one was volcano size! It was at this stage I decided that I'd had enough, and using some very bad language, I told him I was sick of his rages and tantrums, he was nothing but an angry shit. So, I grabbed the coal-bunker and marched off up the road in a very foul mood!

I was so angry with him I seemed to take it out on the road by pounding and stamping it with my feet, and by the time I had stopped cursing and swearing to myself about him, I had covered a few kilometres. I struggled to come to my senses (no comments please) and realised that if I carried on at this pace I would either melt, or end up with sunstroke! That crazy fucker had me wound up like a clock spring! I was starting to feel a bit weird, the heat causing ripples off the tarmac added to my dazed state as I was being slowly baked by the intense heat of the sun, it was time to get into slow down and rest mode, I spotted a town not far away and cut off the main road and headed for it, thinking what refuge it may hold, it reminded me of a couple of my favourite books written by Laurie lee, who had spent some time wandering around Spain, generally not going anywhere in particular but visiting many places, and the first bar I came to I went in and sunk a couple of really cool pints of Spanish beer, boy it was heaven! I then began to calm down a bit and relax, when I was approached by a rough looking Spanish girl who asked if I would buy her a bottle of wine, she was going from one customer to another getting constant refusals, and I decided to follow suit. Soon after the barman tried to tell me in Spanish, she was not a good girl, mucho vino si? (much wine yes)

After relaxing for a while and having a cigarette, I decided that as it was near tea time it may be an idea to look for a hostel, and failing that, I would pitch the tent I had brought for such occasions.

I seemed to wander around the town for an eternity asking directions to a hostel, actually going up and down some of the streets twice! When eventually my persistence paid off when I came to a hostel for the grand sum of about £11 per night. It was a really old place, and the lady owner could possibly have been as old as the building itself. As she spoke no English, and my Spanish is limited, I was afraid my passport would be out of date before she got the details from it, the heat was intense, and the fan that was spinning round slowly did nothing to help the air flow at all. As she got to the end of the registration form she realised she had asked me to sign on the wrong line, imagine my frustration when she began the whole process again, only this time aided by a semi drunk husband! God I was nearly in tears! It is so difficult to keep smiling when your emotions are telling you you're going to have a breakdown!

Eventually, with my passport still in date, I was shown to my room which although small, it was basically what I wanted, a bed, a sink and a table. I had a shave then headed for the communal bathroom for a shower, which had about the same power as the fan in reception. Nevertheless, cold water was what I wanted and the pleasure of fresh cold water slowly spraying me was heaven itself! I then went back to my room to catch up on my journal, before heading out into the street to find a bar, and a cool beer.

And, as if by magic, I am now parked up in said bar with a nice cold beer, and feeling a whole lot better. My thoughts reflect on the past few days and my experience with Wem, and I can now laugh at the events that have happened. Actually, when I think about it the distance covered compared to his ranting and ravings has been well worth it. Again, people watch me writing with inquisitive eyes as I smile gently to myself and scribble away in my travel journal. The girl behind the bar ventures to ask what it is I am writing about, so I briefly tell her the tale about young Jonny back at home in the pub at Bowness on Solway, and how the trip came about, and she is amazed that I have hitched such a distance since leaving home. I start to chat to her and she is typically Spanish, lovely smile and very beautiful, Lots of things have happened since I set off on my journey, and ie had some fantastic experiences, from simply being alone to meeting all kinds of people, and going to different places. The Spanish countryside is beautiful, with butterflies, and Bougainvillea plants hanging over garden walls, and old men propping them up as if frightened to leave they will fall over.

I think the bit I like best about the whole trip is the travelling alone part, ie always enjoyed my own company for as long as I can remember, I sometimes see life like the waltzers at the fairground, nice just to stand and watch, and at times great fun to jump on and join in! or, looked at from another angle, as opposed to its nice to be on your own now and then, I think it's nice to be with people now and then.

I soon slip into daydream mode, and my mind does all sorts of wandering, going back and forth to the many trips abroad I have done on my own, many lovely memories come to mind, then fade as I get another image or thought. This is absolute bliss, I re-enter the earths atmosphere, as the music is turned up loud. Its Friday night and the locals are chatting and socialising so I decide to ring the pub at home, just spoke to father Dave (Jan's dad, as opposed to a character from a t.v. programme) and Andrew Birket,(AKA Keith Chegwin) real good crack to speak to them both, gave them an update on my adventure,

Starting to feel a bit weary now, I didn't realise that I may get a little tired along the way, probably need a holiday to recover! I can't wait to flop into a nice clean bed, I may lie in for a while, In fact I'm totally washed out right now, I think the lack of sleep has finally caught up with me, and so to bed.

After waking up at 9.30.! And 10 hours sleep I get washed and pack up the coal bunker and hit the road once again. I am now in the La Mancha region and I think of Don Quixote, and his faithful manservant Pancho Villa roaming the countryside and waging war on windmills! I wander along in a relaxed pace and enjoy the sights and smells of the Spanish countryside, while I stick my thumb out hoping for a lift. Some of the cars toot their horn as they pass, and I begin to think are they wishing me good luck, or do they want me to get off the side of the road?

Some kilometres later I stop for breakfast, which consists of a ham and cheese toasted sandwich and a very welcome cup of tea, (due to the heat I have decided not to have a glass of ice cold coke as it will not do my stomach much good when I am walking) and now I am sat down it is a bit of an effort to get up again. Eventually I get back on the road and decide it may be a good idea to head for the coast and Alicante. The heat is unreal, and makes me very weary, but I carry on stopping to look at flowers insects and many other things that distract me along the way, sometimes sitting on the coal-bunker while having a cigarette and watching the world go by, and after many kilometres and no lifts I eventually come to a village and a chap at a local café tells me there is not much chance of getting a lift, so I sit outside in the shade, writing and colouring. I then head off again and happen to pass a market and decide to get some of the delicious tomatoes, and fruit on offer, but the stallholder will not let me pay for the tomatoes after I explain to him they are the best in the world and not at all like the ones we get in England. Further up the road and more kilometres covered, I take out some of the tomatoes and sprinkle a little salt and pepper on them and savour the flavour with seeds and juice running down my chin.

Conscious of my arranged meeting with Joe and Tracey in Barcelona I get back on with the business of walking and hitching, and eventually get a lift in a small tipper truck and when I ask the driver to sign the t-shirt he looks oddly at me and asks "Regalo" which in Spanish means gift as he holds it up against himself as if in a clothes shop! but eventually signs it. He seems to think it is something to do with football, so instead of a long winded explanation I say in my best Spanish, Si, which means yes, he seems to like this as he looks over at me now and again and smiles. As we truck along I try to make conversation but find it both difficult and frustrating, we stop here and there for a coffee and I pay, café con leche, coffee with milk and its lovely, I struggle to stay awake as is often the case and after a few hours I am in Alicante and enter a local bar where sat next to me is a drunk Spanish chap busy talking to himself, there is also another chap with a Mohican haircut sat with his chica. He is friendly and keeps smiling and looking over, I point to the beer bottle on the bar and then the drunk chap, and the Mohican says si Espanola hombre mucho barracho, which in my limited Spanish translation means yes the Spanish man is very drunk.

I then go and sit outside and relax, while enjoying the Spanish music filtering from the dusty speakers on the wall, and watch people coming and going. After a while my daydreaming in interrupted by the sound of screaming engines from within the bar so being a petrol head I go and investigate, and to my delight Formula 1 racing is on the telly. So I then fall into conversation with a chap about the racing, not forgetting to mention the names of Spanish and Columbian drivers.

I then make my way into the centre of Alicante, at this stage I am feeling really exhausted, I think this is due to the walking and the temperature, the sun never seems to let up roasting me. After many jumbled conversations I finally get to the centre and spy a large bus station, so decide to exercise my hitching skills with a chap who seems to be of some importance, and after much misunderstanding on both our parts he gets me a free lift on a bus to Benidorm, only the bus doesn't leave for a while, it's not a great distance but I'm glad of the free lift.

So, to fill in some time before the said bus leaves, I put the coal-bunker into a locker and go wandering around looking at the shops, what a relief it is not to have the thing on my back. In one particular area I come across a street almost full of Chinese shopkeepers, it seems a bit strange to hear Chinese people talking away in Spanish to each other, so I linger in shops just to hear them speak, I then came across a most unusual building it looks like a French chateau and has Green ceramic elephants heads on the corners of each floor and lovely features, I get very curious and go to the reception only to be met by what look like security staff who ask me what I want, I explain as best I can and they shout for someone in the office to come and deal with me, and I am then in the company of a very attractive Spanish female with dark hair, and even darker eyes that tempt me to think....... Sorry! who tells me the building is the archive department of the local government, when i comment that it is not what I expected she goes on to tell me it is called de casa de la bruhas, house of the witches, named so because the daughters of the doctor who built it would be dressed in black mourning clothes and sit outside knitting, as their father had sadly committed suicide by throwing himself over the top floor staircase! God she was attractive and it was difficult to keep focused on what she was saying! she also told me it was haunted by the doctor, "anoche es muchas phantismo" at night there are many ghosts! so, after falling in love briefly, I say thank you and leave.

It is now some time in the early hours of the morning, and I have just got off the free bus ride in Benidorm, all the bars are still open and there are lots of people still out sitting at tables talking and drinking, my first impression is that I don't really like the place as it is so busy not only with people, but also the traffic. So I go down a quiet side street and have myself a couple of beers before wandering off and getting into my sleeping bag on some steps and falling asleep for the rest of the night looking very much like a homeless person.
When I woke up it was early morning, so I rolled up the sleeping bag tied onto on to the coal bunker, roughly brushed my teeth I wandered down to the main road and all the seats and the tables are empty, apart from the various early morning bar staff sweeping up and washing down tables and chairs, so I go to a café and have some lovely sweet tea and an omelette in a bread roll for my breakfast, boy did I enjoy that!

Then it was time to head out of town and up the coast road to Barcelona, I got my map out to look at how far I had to go and it was still some distance, even after screwing my eyes up to shrink it still remained, I asked various delivery drivers directions, and a decent sort of a chap gave me a lift to the edge of town and I am now standing in the heat, I spend time thinking about those at home, Jonny and his family, my children Mike, Vicky and

Joe, Tracy, friends in the office and wonder what they are doing as I ratch out a paper plate, plastic cutlery, tomatoes, ham, cheese, salad, and bread for one of my self catering type snacks, washed down with a gulp of warm water! I then have a cigarette as the heat slowly fries me, as I gaze around me at the roadside and enjoy the open space, for some strange reason Laurie Lee comes to mind and his wanderings through Spain, now that would be a trip and a half following his route from southern England and then down through Spain, this day dreaming goes on for some time and I begin to wonder if all this heat has had an effect on me as at times I do feel a bit light headed, do feel free to throw in a sarcastic comment at this point! It is some time since I was dropped off here and the prospect of a lift looks a bit grim at the moment, but as I am meeting Joe my son in Barcelona, I had better stick it out, I sometimes swear and then laugh at the cars, buses, trucks, and stuff that go by as I hold my thumb up at them.

What seemed like a lifetime later, I get a lift in a wagon, the chap speaks at lightning speed, and in amongst his rapidly delivered words I pick up on the word Barcelona, fantastic! So in my best Spanish I say Barcelona bien muchas gracias meaning Barcelona is ok thank you very much. what a fuckin lift! All the way up the coast to Barsa! Yee haa! I've scored, another long distance lift, only this time with a decent stable individual, not like Wem the bad tempered trucker with the cattle container! "you think is fuckin funny yeah?" crazy dude! It's a long time since the truck had seen the showroom, and one of the engine covers was battered and poorly fitted, so for the next few hours we behave as if we are in a shouting competition! I get the distinct impression that he actually owns the truck, as now and again he pats the dashboard or the engine covers affectionately, and smiles at me. It is a fair distance to Barcelona and it's so nice to just sit and look out of the window watching the Spanish coast on our right, and the Mediterranean Sea. I do get tempted at times to ask the driver to let me off here so I can go snorkelling in the lovely turquoise water and stretch out on the sand, but I think it better to stay on board and reach my destination. It's a long way and although I am grateful for the lift I can't help falling asleep now and again, I try to explain as best I can that I have travelled a lot of miles, he smiles sympathetically as though he understands before we pull off the road along the way and go into a truck stop type of cafés for various snacks including ham rolls (Jamon bocadilla) I'm tired and weary but the thrill of the trip and thoughts of Jonny keep me going, the good old kindly driver re-fuels the trusty rusty truck and we are back on the road again, we plough on northwards and the good old thing keeps chugging away, we try to have conversations and at times I'm almost sure we are agreeing with each other just to be polite, I see signs for Tarragona and realise we are nearing my destination, and remember a trip one time starting with a £ 29 flight to Reus, and then hitching, trains, and buses all the way down to Andalusia, sorry, that's another story, and After what seems like an eternity, and many shouting sessions, we finally arrive in Barcelona, we've done few miles together and what a kind chap he truly is, so I try my best in Spanish to show my appreciation, and as I tell the chap that it is a very good truck indeed, he says gracias amigo, hasta luego, meaning see you later, and drops me off in one of the suburbs. I then hoist the coal-bunker up onto my back and wander off down the street wondering how I will get to the centre, and decide to ask some people sitting outside a café, who then point to the ground, so imagining they are telling me to tunnel, I stand and look puzzled at their directions in Spanish and the gestures to the ground when it dawns on me they mean the metro train! So, I go along a couple of streets and discover the underground station. I am now sitting outside a café in the Plaza Catalunya after an un-planned underground tour of the metro system, I saw two girls, one of who turns out to be a teacher and they reassure me this is the right train, which it turned out it wasn't! not to worry, it was a nice conversation, and lots of train changing. Sometime later...... I have been in an Internet café and sent a few e-mails home with my one finger typing skills, it seemed to take forever. Now waiting to meet Joe and Tracey, I can't wait to see him. We set off for a wander around the centre of Barcelona enjoying each others company, and looking in the various shops before going down the rambler, which is a long main street with a central island that has lots of street artists in all sorts of disguises. some of them stand like statues perfectly still until someone drops a few coins into the box at their feet, and then they come to life and do a performance, sometimes frightening those who are near to them . And people applaud and cameras click with great enthusiasm. Some of the costumes are magnificent, ranging from soldiers to clowns, dancers demons and witches.

Joe and I then go back towards the centre and get an ice cream, and sit and watch it all going by, at one stage we come across a busker who is singing the blues, and he is really good at it. We then meet up with Tracey again, and say our goodbyes. I am now at the ferry terminal and going to make enquiries about a free, or discounted trip across to Menorca, as it is the Spanish school holidays there are literally hundreds of students all over the place, waiting for various ferries going to the Balearic Islands as well as along the coast. After making some enquiries, I'm told tonight's ferry to Menorca is full, so decide to wait and see if there has been a cancellation. So, to fill in the time I wander along the harbour to look at the boats and some of the splendid buildings, as there are lots of people about I spend some time apologising for banging into them with the coal-bunker.

After a lovely snack of juicy tomatoes, cheese, and crusty bread, and the company of many sea-gulls, I decide to go back to the office at the ferry terminal to see if there are any cancellations only to discover there are none. So it's looking like a night in Barcelona. I am really hot and sweaty with all the walking around in the heat, and having just caught a glimpse of myself in a shop window, I decide a shave and a shower will do me some good and make me a little more presentable. So I then set off looking for a hostel, only to find the first three I call at are full, I begin to wonder if my Robison Crusoe like appearance is the real reason? But strike lucky at the fourth when the receptionist tells me they have one room

available and that it's a double, well as it's late in the evening and although slightly over budget, I decide to take it. I justify this slight extravagance by deciding that as its probably my last night on the peter pan trip, and the fact I look a bit on the scruffy side, along with the need to get some rest so I go for it, I go up to my room and find it is rather luxurious for a hostel, and un-pack some of my gear on to the bed before having a shave and a deliciously hot shower, which was much needed. I then lay on the bed put on some music and enjoyed the feeling of being clean and getting a good nights sleep, but as the night was not completely over I decide a couple of beers would be a perfect end to the day.
Now sitting at a table outside a bar not far from the hostel with a large beer, and when I say large I mean large! I asked for a Grande cerveca, and was given what I would call a stein. Which is roughly the equivalent of about two pints? And at this stage of the proceedings I don't really care what the waiter brings me.

While sitting drinking from the huge glass I start to write out some more postcards, and then remember I have left my phone at the hostel, so after asking the waiter to look after my drink etc, I go back for it. Then get back to writing in my journal, scribbling on postcards and watching the people wandering by, I get this really good feeling as I have somewhere to spend the night just along the street, I'm all clean and fresh, and looking forward to the comfort of a nice bed. Then something a bit strange happened. I didn't really need my phone, but something made me go and get it, and a few minutes later it rang, it was Lenny Rook from Anthorn asking how

I was, and how the trip was going, how odd as I had not only gone back for the phone, but minutes earlier one of the postcards I had written was to Lenny!

Sometime later, still sitting outside the bar I get talking to Philippe a Frenchman and his two daughters called Oceane, and Gwendolyn. Very nice people they are, so we get more drinks in and carry on talking. Turns out Philippe is a kitchen designer and fitter. Aint it great how you just bump into people and get talking, in fact I sat down at about 10.30 and in no time at all it was 1. 25 in the morning, and we had all enjoyed the relaxing atmosphere as well as the conversation. I then set off to stagger back to the hostel when shortly after I was approached by a street prostitute looking for some late night clients, but I assured her that I had no need for her services, and anyway, my mother was at home waiting for me! So off I went, climbed the stairs to my room, put on some nice tunes and collapsed into bed! Night night.

I didn't wake up until 10.20 which is not like me at all, it must be due to extra rations of Spanish beer and a rather late night, So after brushing my teeth and getting washed I go back to the ferry terminal and test my begging skills on the staff at the booking office. After a lot of questions and me producing the picture of Jonny, along with trying to look sad and dejected, they tell me I can't travel for free but they will give me a discount on my ticket. So, at 5 o'clock the boat sails for Menorca, the last leg of my journey, and with this in mind I am going to spend today just doing nothing and soaking up the atmosphere of the place. Went back to the hostel packed up the coal-bunker and wandered off back to the rambler and parked myself up at a pavement table and ordered myself a beer, I can't wait to get on the boat to Menorca at 5 o'clock, and walk into bar Miami to see the people I had made friends with on previous trips. They are really friendly people and in my view a lot nicer than some of the people I have come across here in Barcelona, in fact to be brutally honest a lot of them lack manners and respect. And at times I have told one or two of them, so there!

But for the moment I am well chilled and relaxed. The end of my trip will soon be here so I sit and reflect on some of the things that have happened, and the people I have met, including Wem the angry Belgian trucker, and I can't help but smile as I wonder where he is at this moment in time. Sometime later I am still sitting here in the rambler sipping cool beer and watching everything pass me by, with absolutely no intention of moving! The feeling of contentment and liberation is awesome. In my book, this is loafing around five star! Later on I loaf off to another bar where I met Dick Turpin who has a job here in Barcelona serving beer and charging the equivalent of £2.50 for a half glass!
After a long slow enjoyable day I am now on board the ferry to Menorca only there has been a slight geographical problem, the boat docks at Ciutadela in the north of the island and not at Mahon in the south as I thought, but as the island is only about thirty miles long it is not a great problem.

For some unknown reason, the ferry company must think everyone is a great television fan, as from where I am sitting there are 9 TV. Screens! So I decide to transfer myself to the bar where there is some nice music playing, I did take this up with the stewardess who informed me the televisions were mostly for the children, I said fine, but what about the adults? She smiled and carried on with whatever she was doing. I was pleasantly amused at the people moving around, as due to the motion of the boat it appeared that everybody was drunk, including me. Sudden impulse to indulge in champagne and strawberries! In fact sitting overlooking the harbour in Mahon with a bottle might well be on the menu this week, what am I saying might? I bloody well will! How emphatic one has become!

Just had a time check, and in about one hour I will be stepping ashore on the isla Bonita, that's beautiful island of Menorca to you and me. Yes yes yes!

I didn't realise we have been at sea for nearly four hours, the time has flown by due to my writing, colouring my small sketches and sticking the various receipts in my journal. Slight interruption here, I have just seen a very very, attractive Spanish woman, no fancy clothes or jewellery, dark longish hair, no makeup, just naturally beautiful, I steel the odd glance, and get rewarded with the most lovely smile, Umm……..

Meanwhile back on earth, just had a look at the sat-nav type of screen on the wall which shows route, distance, time until arrival etc, and in about 40 minutes we should reach Ciutadela. I'm getting a little excited about it all, especially catching up with the people in bar Miami, it's gonna be a howler! I can tell you. Had some great texts off the lads back home all saying very sincere things, Thanks lads, I really appreciate that.

I have just experienced one of the most beautiful sunsets I have ever seen, the sun a huge ball of orange fire slipping slowly over the horizon, and creating little flickers of light on the top of the waves. Nearly beats the sunset I once saw in the Sahara desert, nearly.

Well folks! The bit ie waited for all these miles has finally arrived, I'm here! I've done it! Finally set foot on Menorca, sweaty, scruffy, tired, and immensely happy! So as someone suggested I should chill for a few days.

Soon, after a slow bus ride I am in bar Bananas, a 24 hour place just beside the harbour in Mahon, due to bar Miami being closed, and still scribbling away in my journal, but beginning to feel a little drunk, I think it is a combination of the strong Spanish beer and fatigue. I'm really knackered to be honest, and feel like I could sleep for a week! So with sleep in mind I make my way to the edge of the harbour with a couple of beers, and unroll my sleeping bag, a little while later a chap called Pedro(who I bought an old boat from on a previous trip) passes by in a hummer jeep and toots the horn, and waves, how nice of him.

So now I am settled for the night on the edge of the harbour, got the stereo out and put on some slow relaxing tunes and cracked open a beer, It's difficult to find the right words to describe this feeling, such freedom, no cares at all, complete lack of any responsibility, and the great distance I have covered in completing what I set out to achieve, along with the atmosphere, the lights, and the music, the beer only adds to this carefree feeling, and above all, reaching my goal for Jonny, I slowly drink the beer and my mind just drifts away, I'm drowning in tiredness and my emotions.

After waking up on the harbour side, I open a bottle of water to get a basic wash and to brush my teeth, then pack away my sleeping bag and gather up my belongings and put them into the coal bunker. And then decide to go and look for a hostel, well as I wander down some side streets I hear a voice shouting "Peter" and as I look round I see Miguel, a chap who comes from Columbia who I met here a couple of years ago when he was working in a bar, he remembers me sending him some Tom Jones CDs, and a book he had asked for. It was really good to see him again, and we spent some time talking.
Having just secured a 3 night stay at the hostel Isla, I dump my stuff on the bed, have a shower and go to the bank and the supermarket. Then I decide to just sit and sit.

Sometime later…….. I have just walked into bar Miami, and Janet (the co-owner) hugs and kisses me, and then Andreas her son grabs hold of me like a brother, large hugs all-round! He then introduces me to more people, everyone is friendly and welcoming, its bloody great! So after a few beers I head back to the hostel for a nap as Andreas has said to go and meet him tonight and mentions the word Fiesta, which means party!

Later in the evening I go back to bar Miami, and meet up with Andreas who drags me around the place introducing me to all of his South American friends, and the beers are coming thick and fast!

So, after a session with Andreas and his friends, I only just escaped from being hi-jacked to a local night club, I then get a couple of cans of beer and decide to sit on the balcony at the hostel, and just enjoy the solitude. The music is playing, and the beer is strong (5.4%) and I'm so chilled its un-believable!

Woke up some time mid morning, and lay in bed just daydreaming for a while before getting shaved and showered, and then decided to go to the supermarket to get some supplies in, along with champagne and strawberries, and head to the beach for the afternoon. Now on the bus to Punta Prima, I think it's one of my favourite places on the island, with champagne and strawberries on board as well as bread, cheese, ham, and pate. Aint I living it up? And why not eh? This part is the official end to my journey by way of a little celebration, all for you Jonny!

Now on the beach, after calling into the bar and meeting a chap called Niel, who drives a furniture van around Bishop Auckland, he was amazed when I guessed his accent first time, so we spent some time chatting and having a few beers, before I went onto the beach and opened the champagne and began to slowly eat all the straw berries, and have my picnic of lovely bread, with cheese and ham, Yummy! I then got my snorkelling kit on and went into the sea, it was warm and clear, and the alcohol had certainly helped to regulate my breathing. I was so relaxed and floated around watching the fish darting to and fro, and before long I had drifted almost out to the lighthouse which is about a quarter of a mile from the shore! I slowly finned back to the beach and lay down to relax and was soon asleep on the sand with the warm sun slowly baking me. I woke up sometime later, got all my stuff together, (including the empty champagne bottle) and hopped back on the bus to Mahon. On my way back to the hostel I went into Bar Miami, and was soon in the company of Andreas and the Sud Americanos (South Americans) who began to put some Mexican type music on, and very soon we were back in party mode! Dancing vigoroursly to the sound of guitars and trumpets and buying each other beers like they were going out of fashion! There was much hand shaking and back slapping going on as the party seemed to gather momentum and time slipped by un-noticed as the early evening blended into the night time. And of course the writing got less and less!

Some session last night! In fact at one stage, I was convinced someone had moved the hostel! As try as I might I just couldn't find it at all. I slept the night in a car, and can vaguely remember getting lost in a maze of back streets, I think I went a little crazy on the cerveza with

Andrea's and his friends. What a night! At one stage I virtually got seduced by a Spanish girl called Christina who helps out behind the bar, it was strange as I was writing in my journal she came over to me and asked my name, and I replied Peter Pan. Her face took on this astonished look, and then after having a quick glance around the bar she pulled her top slightly down to reveal a tattoo on her breast, and who was it? Yeah, Peter Pan! I don't know who was more amazed Christina or me! And all the while Andreas and his friends are shouting and giving me some stick as she smiles seductively at me and I begin to melt! as we were talking I explained as best I could how it was so frustrating for me when I wanted to converse in Spanish but had not yet acquired the skills needed, although I am able to speak some basic Spanish, Christina helped me out by producing an English/Spanish dictionary which at one time belonged to her son and proceeded to show me how to use it, as she was at work and carried on serving drinks, I began to try out my new guide to the beautiful Spanish language, tore a page from my travel journal and wrote on it in Spanish " Yo voluntad secuestrar tu " which means " I will kidnap you " and when there was a slack period in her work Christina comes over again to talk, I then slid the piece of paper across to her, she quickly read my message then leaned over the bar put her arms around my neck and pulled me close to her then kissed me fully on the lips! I was astonished and delighted at her response to my romantic gesture which was followed by clapping and hoots of laughter from the customers, I was dizzy with it all.

Surprisingly, the next morning I'm feeling a little better after a lightning visit to the supermarket for fresh supplies, fruit, ham, and delicious tomatoes. Boy can them south Americans party, in fact as a memento they have given me a CD with the guitar music on it, and since being home I have often played it, and it never fails to raise a smile, along with a Spanish love song called Como quiera that seemed to be a particular favourite of Christina's.

At one stage last night, I really felt sorry for one particular chap who was finding it hard to communicate, (no, not through alcohol consumption) but because he didn't know one word of English, but was trying desperately to express himself. So I did try to help him, and after much confusion we arrive at hombres mucho amigable, meaning the men are really friendly, shake hands for the fifth time and say bien, (ok) then carry on jumping around dancing and singing, and as I don't sing fluent Spanish I get by with a feeble attempt at miming the chorus.

Well folks, sadly, it is time to think about going home, so I go to the airport to check if there are any cheap flights to the UK, and there is one tonight, so rather than have to wait until after the weekend I decide to take it. Although being stuck in Menorca is no bad thing, I've had a whale of a time but must get back to work, see my children, and catch up with lots of other stuff, including a forthcoming trip to Japan. So I went back to Bar Miami for the last time to say my goodbyes to Janet, and Andreas, who hugs me heartily and says in broken English, Peter, you my brother, which I found quite moving, and of course to Christina, who insists on giving me a lift to the airport where we embrace and steal a kiss.

So, it's time to sign off for now, I hope you have enjoyed reading about my adventure as much as I have writing about it, not forgetting it has all been for Jonny from Bowness pub.

Adios amigos, Peter Pan.

P.S. Landed back home and rang Dave (Birthday cake neck) Milne at his work to inform him of my completed mission, dumped my gear back in the caravan and Staggered into the village pub at Bowness on Solway to down a few pints while I handed Jonny the signed t-shirt, and chatted with him about my adventures on the trip. Call this crazy, but I have developed a notion to hitch hike to Jamaica. Watch this space!

It's been sometime since I did the trip and began the long task of one fingered typing to get this transcribed from the travel journal onto a computer, and Jonny and me have had many nights talking about the trip with much laughter, sadly Jonathan has left the room so to speak, but he is still very much in our hearts and minds and is often spoken of with much affection by myself and countless others whose life his friendship enhanced.